Black Excellence Affirmations for Women

Positive Affirmations for Queens to Increase Self-Esteem, Happiness, Healing, Confidence, Inspiration, Success, Love, and Sex!

Tasha Tinsley

Contents

Introduction

Hello, my queens! I'm so excited that you've joined me for this exercise in empowerment.

The act of reading, repeating, or listening to affirmations can be transformative! Surrounding yourself with positivity makes you a more positive person. It's that simple.

There has been a ton of research that backs up this idea.

And, if you think about it, you know it's true!

In my personal experience, affirmations have helped me: reclaim my power, find my confidence, trust my instincts, calm the hell down, and live my life to the fullest.

With this project, "Black Excellence Affirmations for Women," I want to take it a step further. I wanted to write affirmations specifically for my people. Black women. Black girls. Mothers. Sisters...

This book helps address our specific challenges.

How should you use this book? Well, in whatever way makes sense to you! Reading or listening to affirmations before bed works for some women. I play affirmations audiobooks in the car when I'm running errands. Some women even exercise with their affirmations in their ears. There is no wrong way to do it!

Welcome. Enjoy. I want you to live your life out loud, and I hope this book helps you do that!

Much love, my queens!

Tasha

Chapter 1

Affirmations for Unwavering Self-Esteem

I am determined.

My confidence is enduring.

I have dignity.

I am steadfast in my self-esteem.

I don't have a big ego.

I am consistent in my strong self-esteem.

I know my worth.

I appreciate myself.

I am worthy of so much.

Self-assurance leads to my success.

I am poised.

My self-esteem's presence is strong.

Unshakeable self-esteem leads me to greatness.

I am steadfast in my self-esteem daily.

I surround myself with others with high self-esteem.

I appreciate myself.

I value myself.

You go, girl!

My self-esteem goes beyond my beauty.

I have unwavering self-love for myself.

I cherish myself with positive, loving thoughts.

High self-esteem is great for my mental health.

I know myself.

I care for myself.

I respect myself.

I accept myself.

I love myself.

My self-esteem leads me to financial security.

My self-esteem leads me to a strong emotional future.

My self-esteem provides me with better physical capabilities.

High self-esteem provides me with a greater walk.

I have well-developed passions and goals and have the realistic motivation to achieve those goals.

Confidence is something I create within myself.

I am allowed to have high expectations.

I am worthy of a beautiful life of peace.

I am well aware of my capabilities.

I am growing into the woman I desire to be each day.

Go me! Go me!

It's not arrogance, it's confidence.

I love the woman in the mirror.

I am the picture of self-love.

I am worthy of love and respect just as I am.

My self-worth is not determined by external validation.

I embrace my strengths and acknowledge my achievements.

I am confident in my ability to overcome challenges.

My value is inherent and not dependent on others' opinions.

I deserve success and will not settle for less.

I am deserving of happiness and fulfillment in all aspects of my life.

Chapter 2

Affirmations for Radiant Happiness

I radiate confidence.

Self-respect radiates from me.

I radiate inner harmony.

My prosperity makes me radiant.

I am brilliant in everything I go through.

I am a gleaming piece of happiness.

My elation glitters everywhere.

I glow through every situation.

My happiness leads to my glow-up.

My bliss is incandescent every day.

Even my rainy days are lustrous.

My bliss is resplendent and overflows.

My delight in myself is shining.

Sunny days are abundant on rainy days.

Happiness leads to other avenues.

Bliss radiates in my daily life.

I have come a long way and grow more every day.

I delight in my progress.

I am the picture of delight.

Enjoyment can be found in my work and passions.

Euphoria and brilliance lead me to better things.

Prosperity is exhilarating, and I've met it.

I walk this Earth with glee.

Joy comes in the morning, noon, and night.

My success is jubilation from all my hard work.

Laughter has healed my soul.

Optimism is an excellent option for accomplishments.

I have a strong peace of mind.

I shine to my win.

I affirm prosperity in myself and those in my circles.

I prioritize my well-being for my happiness.

I set healthy boundaries to maintain my happiness.

I overflow with happiness.

I have delight in conquering my goals.

I am radiant through trials and tribulations.

I deserve happiness.

I deserve success.

I choose happiness.

I am the architect of my happiness.

My happiness is my responsibility.

I am happy with the "smallest" victories.

I find things that make me beam.

I am brilliant.

I rejoice and am glad each day.

I am allowed to be happy.

Healthy and radiant relationships make me happy.

I am happy and blessed.

I am happy to set boundaries.

I have a happy and safe environment.

I feel fabulous.

Chapter 3

Affirmations for Emotional Healing and Renewal

I can heal.

I will get better.

I will continue to grow.

I will continue to flourish.

I will rehabilitate.

I am mending to become better.

The remedy is me.

I am the solution to my problems.

I will fortify myself.

I am working on becoming a better me.

I am rehabbing to be better.

I am renewed.

I am nursing myself to be the best I can be.

I will stop having weak thoughts about myself.

I am deserving of emotional healing.

I release any negative emotions that no longer serve me.

My emotions are valid.

I will rise like the phoenix and renew.

Today is an opportunity for emotional growth.

I let go of past hurts and open myself to new healing experiences.

My emotions guide me towards renewal.

I am in control of how I care for myself.

I trust the process of my emotional healing.

I am worthy of love.

I will not let fear deter me and my healing.

My heart is a space of healing.

I am gentle with myself.

I embrace self-empowerment.

I forgive myself for any past mistakes.

I embrace a brighter future.

My problems will not get the best of me today!

My emotional well-being is a priority.

I trust myself.

I accept myself as I am.

I am surrounded by a supportive and loving community.

I am free from the burdens of the past.

My emotions are a source of strength.

I will let go of past worries.

I will treat myself with love.

I am deserving of renewal.

I let go of laming and embrace my revival.

I am a woman capable of healing from any challenge.

I embrace self-compassion.

I am a work in progress with goals in mind.

I attract positivity into my life.

My heart is open to giving and receiving love freely.

I honor my emotions as I heal.

I am a source of healing for myself and others.

Today, I choose serenity over stress.

I am worthy of renewal.

Chapter 4

Affirmations for Unshakeable Confidence

I am confident and ready.

I handle all situations with ease.

I maintain a positive attitude.

I trust my instincts.

I will have unmovable confidence today.

I am confident in my uniqueness and embrace my individuality.

I have high charisma.

I am a capable and confident individual.

I face uncertainty with courage.

I am secure in what I bring to the table.

I make decisions with confidence.

I am shaped by my growth.

I emit confidence.

Challenges are opportunities for me.

My confidence inspires others.

I can overcome any obstacles in my path.

I am a magnet for success.

My confidence is unshakable.

I am shaped by my resilience and growth.

I am secure in who I am.

I am unwavering in my convictions.

I embrace the unknown with confidence and curiosity.

I am bold.

My self-assurance grows stronger with each day.

Confidence is second nature to me.

I am capable of achieving greatness.

I am ready to embrace the limitless possibilities before me.

I trust my journey.

I am a force to be reckoned with.

My confidence is unyielding.

My confidence empowers me to embrace new experiences.

My confidence empowers me to take risks.

I am fearless.

I trust my decisions and stand firm in my beliefs.

I exude confidence in every aspect of my life.

There are no problems when I am The Equation.

I trust that the universe is conspiring in my favor.

I am the architect of my destiny and build it confidently.

My confidence uplifts those around me.

My confidence inspires those around me.

I have the strength to overcome any adversity.

I am a confident, capable, and resilient woman.

I trust myself to handle any situation with grace and poise.

People are drawn to my confidence.

I am unafraid to pursue my dreams.

I am confident in my ability to create positive change.

I am always guided toward greater and greater success.

I confidently pursue my goals with determination and focus.

Confidence is my ally.

Confidence is mine to own, and I claim it with pride.

Chapter 5

Affirmations for Inner Inspiration and Motivation

I am inspired.

I am motivated.

I motivate others.

I can't be stopped.

My creativity inspires others.

My innovation moves people.

I work with fire in myself.

I have ambition.

I move with passion.

I have an itch for success.

I am a motivating force.

I have drive and ambition.

The determination I have knows no bounds.

I have a sense of purpose.

My sense of purpose pushes me forward.

I have a hankering for success.

I have a sense of purpose.

I provide pep to my friends.

I am the right stuff for the world.

I motivate others easily.

I have the energy to get up and go.

My willpower is unstoppable.

I have the initiative and will use it to proceed.

I have moxie and spirit.

There is a fire in my belly, and it inspires others.

I inspire others easily.

There is no challenge I can't face.

I am enough.

I will work hard for what I want.

There is no obstacle that I can't face.

I will succeed.

I will be better than I was yesterday.

I will be the best that I can be.

There is no stopping my drive.

I have grit; I have hustle.

I have what it takes and then some.

I am woman! I am a goddess!

I am black excellence!

I move with motive.

I move with desire.

I move with gusto!

I can't be stopped.

The mountain will be moved by me.

There is no glass ceiling for me.

I will progress forward and onward.

I have the motivation to strive forward.

I am a go-getter.

I have a newfound warmth after healing my inner self.

I love myself.

I love the journey I'm on to motivate others.

Chapter 6

Affirmations for Unstoppable Success

I am the embodiment of black excellence.

My achievements know no bounds.

I am a force of brilliance.

I stand on the shoulders of greatness, paving the way for success.

I am a trailblazer!

I am breaking barriers.

I am a testament to black excellence.

I am achieving unparalleled success.

I embrace the legacy of black excellence.

My success story is already written.

I am leaving the mark of black excellence in my wake.

I am a living testament to unshakable determination.

I rise above challenges.

I am a vessel of unstoppable success.

My journey is a celebration of black excellence.

I am the architect of my success.

I emit confidence in all I do.

I emit brilliance in all I do.

I am a phoenix rising, fueled by flames.

I emit the essence of black excellence in all I do.

I am a living testament to the resilience of black excellence.

I am a living testament to the brilliance of black excellence.

I am a living testament to the beauty of black excellence.

I am a force of nature.

Unstoppable success is my destiny.

I am creating ripples of success around me.

I am a manifestation of greatness.

I am unstoppable.

Success is not a choice; it is my passion.

Success guides me forward.

Success is not a choice; it is my destiny.

My success is fueled by the flames of black excellence.

I navigate the seas of black excellence.

I am a living testament to the power of black brilliance.

My success journey is a celebration.

I am unstoppable because I stand on the shoulders of giants.

I am a trailblazer, cutting through the darkness with the light.

I am a manifestation of black brilliance.

Unstoppable success is my destiny.

My legacy contributes to the tale of unstoppable success.

I am a symphony of achievement.

I orchestrate my success.

My success journey is not just personal; it is renowned.

My success is rooted in the rich soil of black excellence.

My success is unstoppable.

There is no hurdle I can not overcome.

No wall shall burden me to success.

I will constantly move towards the success I have earned.

My path to success is already set.

No obstacle is too high, and no win is too low.

Chapter 7

Affirmations for Self-Love and Self-Acceptance

I am unique and valuable, just as I am.

I embrace my imperfections because they make me who I am.

I am deserving of love from myself and others.

My worth is not determined by external standards.

I celebrate my strengths and acknowledge my areas for growth.

I am a work in progress, and that's okay.

I treat myself with the same kindness and compassion I offer my friends.

The love I have for myself is high.

I am learning and growing, and that process is something to be proud of.

I love and accept myself as I am today.

I am more than enough just as I am.

I am deserving of respect from myself and others.

I am deserving of kindness from myself and others.

I appreciate the beauty in diversity, including the uniqueness within myself.

I support and encourage myself through challenges.

I choose positive self-talk.

I am proud of my accomplishments, big and small.

I forgive myself for past mistakes.

I contribute to this life in meaningful ways.

I trust in my abilities.

I choose to surround myself with positivity and let go of negativity.

I believe in my potential to achieve great things.

I am a work of art.

I am open to learning more about myself and others.

I take care of my mental and emotional health.

I am not alone. I am accepted just as I am.

I am proud of who I am becoming.

I trust life's process and believe everything is unfolding as it should.

I honor my feelings and express them in healthy ways.

I am capable of achieving my dreams, and I work towards them with determination.

I am a unique combination of talents, interests, and qualities that make me special.

I bounce back from challenges with strength and grace.

I am a positive influence on others.

I choose friends who uplift and support me.

I am proud of my heritage and cultural background.

I am free to be myself.

I let go of the need to conform to others' expectations

I stand up for what I believe in.

I appreciate the journey of self-discovery.

I love contributing my unique perspective.

I am open to trying new things and expanding my interests.

I am patient with myself.

I am responsible for my happiness and choose joy and positivity.

I understand that growth takes time.

I trust in my ability to navigate challenges.

I am a masterpiece in progress.

I am a lifelong learner, curious about the world and my place in it.

I deserve love, and I allow it to flow into my life.

I am a positive force for change.

I am ready to embrace each day.

Chapter 8

Affirmations for Deep Inner Healing

I deserve love and respect.

My past does not define me.

I trust the journey of my life.

I release all negative energy and welcome positivity.

I am a strong woman.

I am a resilient woman.

My self-worth is not determined by external validation.

I forgive myself for any mistakes and learn from them.

I am at peace with my past, present, and future.

I embrace change.

My intuition is a powerful guide.

I am a magnet for miracles.

I am enough just as I am.

I release the need for perfection.

Every challenge is an opportunity for growth and transformation.

I am unique and valuable in my own way.

My body is a vessel of strength.

I am free of self-doubt and insecurity.

I am open to receiving love.

I choose peace and harmony.

I inspire myself and others.

I will not be a people pleaser.

I am the architect of my life.

My inner beauty radiates outward.

I release fear.

I am surrounded by love.

I am grateful for the lessons that have shaped me into who I am today.

My energy positively influences those around me.

I trust the timing of my life.

I honor my emotions.

I release the need to control everything.

I am a creator of positive change in my life.

My heart is open to giving and receiving love unconditionally.

I embrace growth with an open heart.

I celebrate ALL of my achievements.

I attract positivity effortlessly.

I let go of past traumas.

I choose joy and happiness.

I attract positive relationships that nurture and empower me.

My inner strength and resilience are boundless.

I am a powerful creator.

I am at peace with my body, mind, and soul.

I express my authentic self.

I trust the process of life.

I release guilt and shame.

I am a goddess of love.

I am the captain of my ship.

I approve of myself.

My inner child is safe, loved, and nurtured.

I am a vessel of creativity.

Chapter 9

Affirmations for Empowerment and Resilience

I give myself a stamp of approval.

I am blessed in adversity.

My mind is flexible.

My flexibility leads me to success.

I am resilient in every aspect of my life.

I permit myself to live with set boundaries.

My success has my seal of approval.

I give myself a thumbs-up often.

Conflict does not come in adverse moments.

Flexibility has led me to blessings.

Adaptability leads to longevity.

I am a force of nature.

My strength is greater than any challenge I may face.

I trust in my abilities.

I am the architect of my destiny.

Challenges are growth opportunities.

I shape my reality with intention.

I am confident in my abilities.

I stand tall in the face of adversity.

My resilience is a testament to my inner fortitude.

I empower those around me.

I turn obstacles into stepping stones on my path to success.

I trust in my capacity to learn and adapt.

I am a warrior.

I am not defined by setbacks.

I deserve success.

I choose to rise above negativity.

I create my own narrative.

I am a leader for the people.

Big and small achievements lead to success.

I honor my journey.

I am a woman of substance, worth, and unwavering resilience.

I trust the wisdom within me.

I am an empowered woman.

I radiate confidence.

I am a catalyst for positive change.

I am fully equipped to handle life's uncertainties.

I face challenges with a calm and focused mind.

I am capable of achieving anything I set my mind to.

I do not break during storms.

I trust the journey, even when I cannot see the entire path.

My inner strength is a constant source of inspiration.

I am bold.

I attract positivity, strength, and resilience into my life.

I am a survivor.

I am unapologetic.

I am a reservoir of resilience.

I embrace change with open arms.

I navigate challenges with resilience.

Chapter 10

Affirmations for Love and Relationships

Our love is a celebration of us.

We embrace our love and unique connection.

We are partners in love.

Our love is a powerful affirmation in itself.

With each passing day, our bond deepens.

We are creating a love that stands the test of time.

Through the highs and lows, our love remains steady.

Our connection is strong because of our passion for each other.

Our love is a legacy.

With each sunrise, our love is reborn.

We are architects of our love story.

Our love is a journey.

We are building a foundation of trust.

Our love remains unshakeable through challenges.

We make communication a pillar in our relationship.

Our love language is shared laughter.

Every embrace is a reminder of the love we share.

Our love is an affirmation of the beauty within our souls.

To us, respect is the thread that weaves a pattern of lasting connection.

Our love is a flame that burns intensely.

We cultivate a love that blossoms with shared values and dreams.

We have created a lighthearted bond through our joy of laughter.

Our love is a collaboration of trust, intimacy, and action.

Our love remains a constant source of strength and comfort.

We are encouraging each other to reach new heights.

Respect and admiration are the shared values that bind us together.

Our love echoes far and outward.

We appreciate the beauty in our differences.

Our love is a sanctuary.

Through challenges, our love remains resilient.

Our relationship is built on trust and clear understanding.

We shine brightly with the warmth that is our love.

Our love is a powerful force.

We are a team, and our goal is everlasting love.

Our love is full of compassion, understanding, and shared growth.

Communication and love create a pattern of enduring connection.

We celebrate our shared heritage.

Our love remains unyielding.

Our love story is vibrant and joyous.

Our love is a melody -- The best song on the charts.

We are partners in joy and abundance.

Our love is a testament to the beauty within our hearts.

We are in this together.

No one can come between us and our love.

Our love is the beat, and we are the dancers.

This love is a collaborative effort.

We are builders in this journey together.

In our relationship, each shared experience is a masterpiece.

Our love remains constant between us.

Chapter 11

Affirmations for Unleashing Your Creative Spirit

I am ready to unleash my unique ideas into the world.

My creative spirit flows effortlessly.

Each day, I draw inspiration from my experiences.

I trust in my creative instincts.

The power of my creative mind knows no bounds.

I embrace turning obstacles into opportunities.

I am a source of limitless ideas.

I am illuminating the world with my artistic brilliance.

I unlock its potential with every thought.

I recognize that each step of life is a vital part of my artistic journey.

The canvas of my life is painted with the vibrant colors of my creative energy.

I trust the ebb and flow of my creative rhythm.

Creativity is my superpower, and I wield it well.

My mind nurtures ideas into magnificent creations.

I celebrate my creative victories, both big and small.

I move with grace, expressing my true self through artistic expression.

I am lighting the path for others to explore their own artistic potential.

I welcome the muse; it enhances my creative spirit.

I am a creator of beauty.

Each moment is an opportunity for creative expression.

I am a visionary.

My creative spirit is overflowing.

I release any self-doubt that hinders my creative flow.

I trust the process of creation.

Creativity is my ally.

I am proud of the unique perspective I bring to the world.

I am using my creative gifts to inspire and uplift others.

I am a catalyst for positive change.

Today, I chose to stroke my creative intentions.

I am discovering new facets of my artistic self.

I am carving pathways to new and exciting possibilities.

I know that my ideas have the power to transform.

I trust in the divine inspiration that guides me.

I am a beacon of creativity.

The world is my canvas.

I am attracting creative ideas and opportunities into my life.

I embrace the beauty of imperfection.

My creative spirit is a flame that burns brightly

I welcome the unknown with open arms.

I am a force to be reckoned with when it comes to creativity.

My creativity knows no limitations.

I am a conduit for artistic energy.

I break free from any self-imposed constraints and soar to new heights.

I am a vessel of inspiration.

My creativity is a source of empowerment.

I trust that in the process of creative incubation, the beauty will be revealed.

I allow the creative energy to flow through me and into my creations.

I infuse my work with passion.

I radiate creativity, and it shows in my work.

Each day, I strive for new ways to be creative.

Chapter 12

Affirmations for Inner Strength and Empowerment

I permit myself a stamp of approval.

Despite adversity, I am blessed.

Flexibility is one of my strengths.

Success comes from my flexibility.

In every aspect of my life, I am resilient.

The boundaries I set for myself allow me to live a healthy life.

Success is my seal of approval.

My thumbs-up is often a source of pride for me.

Conflict does not consume me.

Blessings have come my way because I have been flexible.

Longevity is fostered through adaptability.

Nature's force courses through me.

Beyond any challenge, my strength prevails.

I place trust in my innate abilities.

The mastermind behind my fate, I am.

Growth unfolds within challenges.

Intentionally, I mold my reality.

Assurance fills me, knowing my capabilities.

Unyielding, I stand tall amidst adversity.

Inner fortitude is showcased through my resilience.

Those around me find empowerment in my presence.

I transform obstacles into stepping stones, paving my path to success.

Trusting in my ability to learn and adapt, I forge ahead.

Warrior spirit courses through my veins.

I transcend setbacks; they do not define me.

Success is rightfully mine; I am deserving.

Opting for positivity, I ascend beyond negativity's grasp.

I author my own narrative, shaping my destiny.

As a leader, I stand for the people's empowerment.

Success stems from both significant and minor achievements.

My journey is honored, and each step leads toward success.

Substance, worth, and unyielding resilience define me as a woman.

The wisdom within me is a trusted guide.

I embody empowerment as a woman.

Confidence emanates from my being.

A positive change catalyst, I am.

Life's uncertainties are met with my complete readiness.

Challenges are approached with a composed and focused mind.

Anything I set my mind to, I am fully capable of achieving.

Unyielding in storms, I remain unbroken.

Trusting the journey, even when it's unclear, is my strength.

A constant wellspring of inspiration, my inner strength.

Boldness defines my character.

Positivity, strength, and resilience naturally gravitate towards me.

A survivor's spirit resides within me.

Unapologetically, I stand in my truth.

Resilience flows abundantly, a reservoir within me.

Change is embraced with arms wide open.

Resilience guides me as I navigate through challenges.

Chapter 13

Affirmations for Charismatic Communication

My words carry weight and impact.

I speak with clarity and confidence.

I listen attentively to understand, not just to respond.

I effortlessly connect with others.

I express myself with authenticity.

I express myself with sincerity.

I embrace the art of storytelling to captivate my audience.

I communicate with purpose and intention.

My body language complements and enhances my verbal communication.

I choose words that inspire and uplift those around me.

I am a master of non-verbal communication.

I can connect with diverse audiences.

My charisma shines through every interaction.

I am a skilled communicator.

I create an inclusive and inviting environment.

I express gratitude and appreciation through my words.

My words build bridges of understanding and connection.

I communicate assertively yet respectfully.

I convey ideas with simplicity and elegance.

I am a confident communicator.

I foster positive energy through my words.

I use humor to lighten the mood.

My communication is a reflection of my inner strength.

I engage in active listening to truly comprehend others' perspectives.

I communicate with warmth and approachability.

My words inspire trust and build rapport.

I am a source of encouragement and support through my words.

I cultivate an uplifting atmosphere through my words.

I choose diplomacy and tact in all my interactions.

I am an effective communicator, making complex ideas easy to understand.

My words have the power to motivate and inspire action.

I convey enthusiasm and passion through my communication.

I speak with conviction and authenticity.

I am open-minded and receptive to different viewpoints.

I express myself with grace and poise.

My communication reflects my genuine interest in others.

I am a confident and charismatic speaker.

I communicate with a perfect balance of confidence and humility.

I choose words that create harmony.

I am mindful of my tone.

I am a clear and concise communicator.

My communication style fosters a positive and collaborative atmosphere.

I express gratitude and acknowledgment freely.

I strive for positive and uplifting conversations.

I effortlessly navigate conversations with grace and ease.

My words create positive energy around me.

I express myself assertively without being confrontational.

I choose words that build and mend.

I am a communicator that leaves a lasting impression on others.

My communication skills continually evolve.

Chapter 14

Affirmations for Building Loving Relationships

Love flows effortlessly between us.

Our connection deepens with each passing day.

I am grateful for the love we share.

We strive to communicate openly and honestly.

I am committed to nurturing our love.

Our relationship is a source of joy and fulfillment.

We support and uplift each other.

Love and understanding guide our actions.

I cherish the unique qualities that make us a perfect match.

I will overcome challenges with love.

Our love grows stronger daily.

We are deserving of a healthy and loving relationship.

Our partnership is built on trust and mutual respect.

We create a safe and supportive space for each other.

I express love through words and actions.

I am open to receiving and giving love freely.

Our love is a beautiful journey of growth and discovery.

We are patient and caring.

Love is the foundation of our shared dreams.

We celebrate both our similarities and differences.

I am committed to creating lasting memories together.

Our laughter and joy create a positive atmosphere.

I appreciate the small gestures.

Love is the guiding force in our relationship.

I am a source of comfort for my partner.

We navigate challenges with resilience.

Our relationship is a sanctuary of love and acceptance.

I choose kindness and compassion.

Love is our key, and our hearts remain unlocked.

Our love guides us through life's journey.

Today, I will love in diverse ways.

We communicate our needs and desires with empathy.

I am worthy of a healthy relationship.

Love is the foundation.

Our connection is open and honest communication.

I am grateful for the laughter we share.

Our relationship is a beautiful dance of give and take.

Love radiates from our hearts.

We create a haven of love, understanding, and acceptance.

I am a loving and supportive partner.

Our love is a powerful force that conquers all.

I choose forgiveness and understanding in moments of difficulty.

I am deserving of a healthy relationship.

Love is the music, and we dance to it nightly.

Our love is the brightest flame.

I am grateful for the love that surrounds us.

We maintain intimacy in our relationship.

Love is the anchor that keeps us grounded in times of uncertainty.

I am open to receiving and giving love unconditionally.

Our love is key, and we give unconditionally.

Chapter 15

Affirmations for Goal Achievement and Ambition

I am focused and determined to achieve my goals.

Each day, I take steps towards my dreams.

My goals are within reach.

I have aspirations and intend to achieve them.

I believe in my ability to achieve anything I set my mind to.

Every step I take brings me closer to my goals.

I am committed to my vision.

I welcome challenges as opportunities.

I celebrate my big and small achievements.

I am disciplined and dedicated to reaching my goals.

My goals align with my values.

I attract success into my life.

I am unstoppable.

I manifest my success into reality.

I am confident in my ability to overcome obstacles.

I am deserving of the success that comes with achieving my goals.

I turn setbacks into comebacks, learning and growing along the way.

My ambition is something to be admired.

My persistence is a crucial factor in my success.

My calling is to succeed.

I have the power to create the life I desire through my goals.

I am committed to consistent and positive actions.

I attract the resources needed to achieve my goals.

My mindset is aligned with my goals.

I am worthy of the success that comes my way.

Challenges are stepping stones to my ultimate success.

I am a goal-setter.

Each day, I am closer to realizing my dreams.

I create my own opportunities.

I follow through with purpose and dedication.

I am fueled by a passion to turn my dreams into reality.

I attract positivity in my pursuit of goals.

I attract resilience in my pursuit of goals.

I have determination in pursuit of my goals.

I believe in the power of my dreams.

My goals inspire me to strive for excellence in all that I do.

I am a goal achiever.

I am persistent.

Success is my constant companion.

My goals are the roadmap to my future.

I adjust my strategies to overcome obstacles.

My dedication to my goals strengthens my resolve.

I am ready to achieve my goals.

I am grateful for the lessons life brings.

I attract success effortlessly into my life.

My goals reflect my purpose.

My goals are the stepping stones to greatness.

I trust in my ability to create a successful and fulfilling life.

I am worthy of the abundance in my life.

I pursue my goals wholeheartedly.

I am fully capable of achieving all my goals.

Chapter 16

Affirmations for Emotional Balance and Well-Being

I am in tune with my emotions.

Each breath I take brings calmness and serenity to me.

I allow peace to flow through me.

I foster emotional well-being.

I can navigate life's challenges with grace.

My emotions guide me toward self-discovery.

I choose positivity and joy in every moment.

I am surrounded by love and support.

I am finding peace in the present moment.

I appreciate the beauty in every experience.

I am free from the weight of past burdens.

Today is a new beginning.

I release fear and anxiety.

I am a beacon of peace.

My emotional well-being is a priority.

I replaced my fears with confidence and calmness.

I forgive myself for any perceived shortcomings.

I find joy in the simple pleasures that life offers me.

I am grounded and centered.

I allow myself to feel and express my emotions in a healthy way.

I breathe, knowing that everything unfolds as it should.

I release negativity and welcome positivity into my heart.

I am at peace with my past, present, and future.

I am surrounded by loving and supportive energy.

I create a sanctuary within myself.

I embrace my imperfections.

I adapt to life's changes with grace and ease.

I choose to focus on the positive aspects of any situation.

I am mindful of my thoughts.

My emotions are like clouds; they pass, and I remain grounded.

I trust my intuition to guide me.

I am worthy of all the good that life has to offer.

I release the need for perfection.

I am a reservoir of inner peace.

I am open to receiving and giving love.

I draw from my well-being in moments of need.

I allow my feelings to flow freely without attachment.

I can navigate life's ups and downs with equanimity.

I am grateful for the lessons that challenges bring.

I am unshaken by external circumstances.

I release the need to control everything.

I am a vessel of love and compassion.

I choose thoughts that nurture my well-being and elevate my spirit.

I am savoring the richness of each experience.

I am uplifting myself and those around me.

I know that challenges lead to growth and expansion.

I forgive myself.

Every challenge I face is an opportunity for personal development.

Today, I choose peace and tranquility.

I am harmonious and balanced with my emotions, mind, and spirit.

Chapter 17

Affirmations for Spiritual Growth and Inner Peace

I choose peace over worry.

I release any stress with every breath.

I let go of the need to compare myself to others.

I am grounded.

I let go of past grievances and open my heart to forgiveness and peace.

I am centered.

I am at peace with who I am.

I am at peace with the present moments.

I am a source of calm.

I release the need for perfection and embrace the beauty of imperfection.

My breath keeps me in a place of inner peace.

I focus on the peace of the present.

I am a peacemaker.

I am at peace with my past, present, and future.

I create a space of serenity within my mind.

I remove the feeling of doubt in my life.

I am a reservoir of inner peace and share it with those around me.

I find solace in silence, nurturing my inner peace.

I am at peace with the ebb and flow of life's natural flow.

I am present in the moment, savoring the peace it brings.

I release tension from my body.

I am a creator of peace.

I release the need to control everything and trust in the natural flow of life.

I am a calm and steady force.

I am a reservoir of inner peace, drawing from it in times of need.

I find peace in my uniqueness.

I protect my peace from external influences.

I am grateful for moments of stillness.

I choose to respond to challenges with a calm and peaceful min

I contribute peace and compassion to the world.

I am a draw for positive energy.

I embrace stillness.

I choose thoughts and actions that cultivate peace within myself and others.

I bring serenity wherever I go.

I am centered and composed.

I am a calm and collected individual, even amid chaos

My presence brings peace to those around me

I am a source of calm strength.

I am mindful of my thoughts.

I am a believer in the power of peace.

I am at ease with my path and my choices.

I let go of the need for constant validation.

I choose to protect my inner peace.

I am a vessel of peace.

I am peaceful. I choose this over chaos.

I am a cultivator of inner peace.

I will maintain my inner peace.

I am at peace with the uncertainties of life.

I spread peace and its influence wherever I go.

I am a peaceful soul, contributing to a world that longs for harmony.

Chapter 18

Affirmations for Attracting Abundance and Prosperity

Abundance flows effortlessly into my life.

I attract prosperity and success.

I attract wealth with every positive thought.

I am open to receiving in abundance.

Prosperity is my goal.

I release all resistance to abundance in my life.

I am grateful for the abundance that surrounds me.

I attract lucrative opportunities with ease.

My mindset is aligned with the energy of prosperity.

I am attracting wealth from all directions.

I deserve to be fulfilled in life.

My actions create a constant flow of prosperity.

I am open to wealth and abundance.

Abundance is my north star.

I am financially free.

I am a prosperous being.

Money comes to me effortlessly.

I am a target for good fortune.

I will be abundant in all forms.

I embrace prosperity in all areas of my life.

Wealth and success are natural outcomes for me.

I am worthy of all the abundance the universe has to offer.

I attract wealth and prosperity with every breath I take.

Money flows to me easily.

I am open to receiving unexpected streams of income.

I am a conscious creator of my financial reality.

Prosperity is for me, and I welcome it with open arms.

I am grateful for all that is constantly flowing into my life.

Prosperity manifests in my life.

I am aligned with the energy of abundance.

The universe is conspiring to bring me prosperity and wealth.

I am and will continue to build my wealth.

My bank account is growing rapidly.

I am open to the infinite possibilities.

I release all limiting beliefs about money and welcome abundance.

I am a vessel for prosperity.

Every dollar I spend comes back to me multiplied.

I am worthy of all the success life has to offer.

I attract financial opportunities.

I allow prosperity to flow freely.

I am open to receiving prosperity from all sources.

Money is a positive force in my life.

I am financially abundant.

My prosperity benefits others.

I attract wealth effortlessly.

I release any blocks to receiving wealth.

Prosperity flows to me in loads of abundance.

I am grateful for the prosperity that flows into my life.

I attract abundance with no effort.

I am grateful for my life and the prosperity I have gained.

Chapter 19

Affirmations for Intimate Connection and Fulfillment

I am present in our intimate connection.

Our love deepens with every shared moment.

I cherish the closeness we share.

I am open to exploring new intimacy with my partner.

Our connection nourishes our souls.

I communicate my desires openly.

I create a space for vulnerability, fostering a deeper emotional connection.

I am attentive to my partner's desires, creating a harmonious intimacy.

Our physical closeness enhances our intimacy.

I express love through both words and physical affection.

I am attuned to my partner's desires.

I am grateful for the passion and intimacy we share.

I listen to my partner's needs.

I prioritize quality time for my partner.

I create a loving and nurturing environment for our connection to thrive.

I appreciate the uniqueness that makes our bond unique.

I communicate love through touch.

I want our intimacy to deepen.

Our intimacy is a beautiful dance of love and connection.

I express my love and desire for my partner with sincerity.

I am mindful of creating a safe and comfortable space for intimacy.

I am attuned to my partner's needs.

Our intimacy is a sacred and evolving journey.

I am open to expressing and receiving love in meaningful ways.

I prioritize quality time for our connection.

I am committed to fostering a loving and intimate relationship.

I am attuned to the love language of my partner.

I am grateful for the intimacy between us.

I am receptive to my partner's desires.

I create moments of intimacy that strengthen our bond.

Our physical closeness deepens our emotional understanding.

I communicate my love through actions.

I am open to deepening our intimate connection.

I prioritize our emotional well-being in our relationship.

I am grateful for the deep connection we share.

I am savoring the intimacy we create together.

I express my love through tender and affectionate gestures.

I embrace enhancing our intimacy.

Our connection is a blend of emotional depth and physical closeness.

I am open to evolving our relationship.

I express my love and desire with authenticity and passion.

I am receptive to my partner's cues.

I create an environment of trust and safety for us.

I communicate my love through touch.

I am open to the transformative power of our intimate connection.

I express my love through words and actions.

I enjoy our physical intimacy and touch.

I love you.

I prioritize the sacred bond of intimacy.

Our intimacy is a beautiful and evolving journey that we navigate together.

Chapter 20

Affirmations for Sensual Confidence and Pleasure

I am worthy of experiencing pleasure and sensuality.

My body is a source of pleasure and delight.

I embrace and celebrate my sensuality.

I am confident in expressing my desires and needs.

Sensual pleasure is a natural and positive part of my life.

I radiate confidence in my own skin.

I am deserving of pleasure and fulfillment in all aspects of my life.

I honor and cherish my body.

I am allowing myself to fully experience pleasure.

I embrace the beauty of my desires.

Pleasure is mine to have.

I allow myself to savor moments of sensual bliss.

I release any shame associated with my sensuality.

My sensuality is a powerful force in my life.

I am open to exploring new dimensions of pleasure.

I am confident in expressing my sensuality.

I take joy in learning new pleasures.

I take time to indulge in activities that bring me sensual joy.

I am free to express my sensuality without judgment.

I am a sensual goddess.

I am confident in my own allure.

I respond to my body's desires with love.

I am comfortable and confident in my own sensuality.

I embrace my body's sensuality.

I indulge in pleasurable experiences.

I am deserving of sensual pleasure.

I claim the sensual essence that makes me uniquely me.

The pleasure I see is empowering.

I am open to receiving pleasure in all areas of my life.

I prioritize self-care and sensuality in my daily routine.

I am confident in expressing my desires.

My sensuality is a sacred vow I have.

I am deserving of love.

I am deserving of pleasure.

I am deserving of fulfillment.

I welcome pleasure with open arms.

I take joy in being sensual with my partner.

I honor and respect my body.

The joy I feel from personal pleasure is powerful.

I release myself with pleasure often.

I am open to receiving and giving pleasure with authenticity.

I release any inhibitions and allow myself to fully enjoy sensual experiences.

I am deserving of pleasure.

I celebrate the sensuality that resides within me unapologetically.

My body is a temple of sensuality.

I exude confidence and allure.

I trust in myself to give me pleasurable experiences.

I am soft and supple.

I take pride in the sensual nature I exude.

I am confident, sexy, and powerful.

Conclusion

Thanks so much for spending this time with me. I hope "Black Excellence Affirmations for Women" has created some positive changes in your life. It's my mission to empower people, and I hope we accomplished that together.

If you enjoyed this book, please leave a review. They are wildly helpful, and good reviews expose us to a larger audience.

With all my love and respect,

Tasha